Deep Down in the waste pipe,
Where the stinky stuff goes,

You can find Tummy Bug,
By his belly that glows.

He likes grubby places,
And plays in dirt and grime,

It may not sound much fun,
The way he spends his time!

What's that? Tummy Bug can't be seen?
Living on things that aren't very clean,

He likes to sneak into your tummy,
And make it feel strange and funny!

"I like to play in grimy bins",
he says, with a wink,

"That has mouldy meat and
rotting food that makes it stink!

I build camps with smelly cabbage leaves,
I build tunnels with empty old tins,

I really feel at home,
In a dirty, smelly bin!"

"Peek-a-boo!" says Jeff the cat,
looking in the bin,

"Come on in!" squeals Tummy bug
with a sly grin,

When Jeff hears this,
he starts to preen and purr....

"You can't get me Tummy Bug,
Because I lick clean my fur!"

Tummy Bug grunts, "Not today Jeff,
I might not get you today,

By cleaning your fur, you will keep
me away!"

"See me sail like a pirate
On the dirty water's slime,

Cruising with mouldy sharks,
Made from grease and scaly lime!"

"I also swim through soured milk
that's become all smelly,

If you drink one of these
you'll get an aching belly!"

Splosh! goes the water
filling up the sink
Making soapy bubbles
coloured blue and pink.

"You can't get me Tummy Bug!"
Sings little Harry Sands,
"I use soap and water,
When I wash clean my hands!"

"I can hide in meat that's too old or raw,

I can even hide on an unwashed floor!"

I like to follow dirty footprints,
Like an explorer in the jungle,

I track down rotting food
and tasty bits, Like rice pops,
bacon or fruit crumble!"

Swoosh! goes the mop across the floor

Everything's squeaky clean,
from sink to the door

"You can't get me Tummy Bug!"
Chuckles the happy Mrs. Beamer,

While washing her kitchen
with a household cleaner.

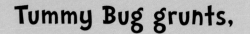
Tummy Bug grunts,
"Not today Mrs Beamer! I might not get you today,

By cleaning your kitchen you will keep me away!"

"I can hide on muddy boots,
shoes and clogs,

I can hide on hands that pat dirty dogs

I can hide on mucky fingers
you like to lick,

But remember, I can make you
feel quite sick!"

"When I play on dirty dogs
I never get nervous

Because I'm the ringmaster
of a flea circus!"

Now, Tummy Bug, is not
a very clean fellow,

He has a swirling tummy
of green and yellow,

He makes your tummy
ache and churn,

To keep him away,
listen and learn ...

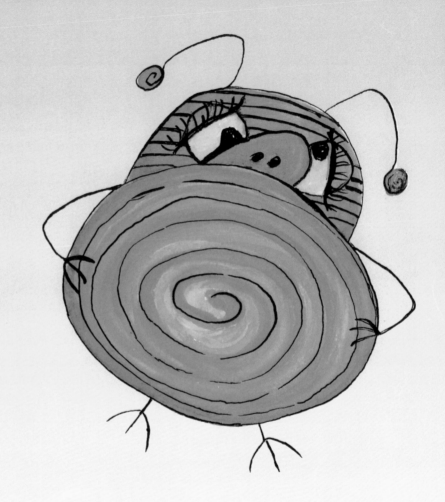

Tummy Bug hates soap
or anything that's clean,

He doesn't like washed hands or
fingernails that gleam!

Wash your hands properly
After using the loo

Wash your hands properly
Before eating food too

Remember to do this every day
And this will make him go away!

Please visit again, as there are plenty more
of Life's Little Bugs to meet!
Find out which ones might be near you right now!